SCHOOL
OF THE
AMERICAS

José Rivera

BROADWAY PLAY PUBLISHING INC
224 E 62nd St, NY, NY 10065
www.broadwayplaypub.com
info@broadwayplaypub.com

SCHOOL OF THE AMERICAS
© Copyright 2007 by José Rivera

1st printing: Apr 2007. 2nd printing: Aug 2010.
I S B N: 978-0-88145-336-2

Book design: Marie Donovan
Word processing: Microsoft Word
Typographic controls: Ventura Publisher
Typeface: Palatino
Printed and bound in the U S A

SCHOOL OF THE AMERICAS was commissioned by South Coast Rep, Martin Benson and David Emmes, Artistic Directors.

SCHOOL OF THE AMERICAS received its world premiere on 6 July 2006 in a co-production between The Joseph Papp Public Theater (Oskar Eustis, Artistic Director; Mara Manus, Executive Director) and the Labyrinth Theater Company (Philip Seymour Hoffman and John Ortiz, Artistic Directors; Steve Asher, Executive Director The cast was as follows:

LUCILA CORTES . . . . Karina Arroyave
JULIA CORTES . . . . Patricia Velasquez
LIEUTENANT FELIX RAMOS . . . . Felix Solis
FIRST ARMY RANGER . . . . Raul Castillo
SECOND ARMY RANGER . . . . Nathon Lebron
RADIO VOICES . . . . Carlo Alban
CHE GUEVARA . . . . John Ortiz

Director . . . . Mark Wing-Davey
Scenic design . . . . Andromache Chalfant
Costume design . . . . Mimi O'Donnell
Lighting design . . . . David Weiner
Sound design . . . . Rob Kaplowitz
Animal trainer . . . . William Berloni
Fight choreographer . . . . Qui Nguyen
Vocal coach . . . . Andrea Haring
Production stage manager . . . . Damon W Arrington

This play would not have been possible without *Compañero: The Life and Death of Che Guevara* by Jorge G Castañeda, *Che Guevara: A Revolutionary Life* by Jon Lee Anderson, and the documentary film *The Bolivian Diaries*.

Additional thanks to Sona Tatoyan, Camilia Sanes, Joe Quintero, Misi Lopez-Lecube, Johnny Sanchez, Javi Mulero, Gary Perez, Lidia Ramirez, Onahoua Rodriguez, Rene Rivera, John Ortiz, Joselyn Reyes, Mel Nieves, Jason Olazabal, Jo Bonney, Alexa Scott-Falherty, Felix Solis, The LAByrinth Theatre Company, Rachel Esparza, Brandon Jones, James Rodriguez, Phillip Boyle, Nick Mangano, Nicholas Gallegos, Vanessa Rios y Valles, The Garson Theater Company, Yul Vazquez, Russell Jones, Andrea Ciannavei, Jessica Kahler, John Cancado.

CHARACTERS & SETTING

Lucila Cortes
Julia Cortes
Lieutenant Felix Ramos
First Army Ranger
Second Army Ranger
Radio Voices
Che Guevara

Time: October 7-9, 1967

Place: La Higuera, Bolivia

ACT ONE
Scene One: JULIA's house. Night
Scene Two: Outside the school house. The next morning

ACT TWO
Inside the school house. That afternoon

Intermission

ACT THREE
Inside the school house. The next day

ACT FOUR

Scene One: JULIA's house. Later that day
Scene Two: Inside the school house. That night

...she knew she had an exquisite audience, one which demanded not forms, but the marrow of forms.
—Lorca

I had a thought for no one, but your ears;
That you were beautiful and that I strove
To love you in that old high way of love;
That it had all seemed happy, and yet we'd grown
As weary-hearted as that hollow moon.
—Yeats

...almost without speaking, they went ahead like sleepwalkers through a universe of grief.
—Marquez

"Che" is fairly intellectual for a "Latino".
—C I A Biographic and Personality Report, 1958

For Walter

ACT ONE

Scene One

(La Higuera, Bolivia. Night, October 7, 1967)

(JULIA CORTES's house: one room serving as the living room, dining room and primitive kitchen.)

(White walls, minimal rustic furniture, wooden floors, poor. Religious prints on the walls. Crucifixes and images of Jesus. A radio. Some books. Windows reveal a dark night.)

(JULIA, thirty-one, and her sister LUCILA CORTES, thirty-four, listen to the radio.)

(JULIA is strong, with black hair and deep-set eyes.)

(LUCILA's hair is long and wild. She is chronically sick and weak.)

FIRST RADIO VOICE: *...El ejército del Presidente Barrientos es actualmente activo en varias frentes: construyendo caminos en regiones difciles y areas rurales aisladas, distribuyendo los asuntos instruccionales anti-guerrilleros, y otorgando los titulos a campesinos que de uno o otro modo carecen de tierras. Reflejando asi un esfuerzo de gran importancia personal al gobierno del Presidente Barrientos, el ejército reparte suministros y materiales a las escuelas de areas rurales mas necesitadas que se encuentran tristemente abandonadas y privadas de cualquier ayuda. Esta es la Radio Pio Doce.*

(JULIA turns off the radio.)

JULIA: *¡Ay, qué tonteras!*

FIRST RADIO VOICE: ...the army of President Barrientos is currently active on a number of fronts: building roads in difficult and isolated rural regions, distributing anti-guerilla instructional matter and granting land titles to otherwise landless peasants. Reflecting an effort of great personal importance to President Barrientos, the army is also giving out much-needed school supplies in these sadly deprived rural areas. This is Radio Pio Doce.

(JULIA turns off the radio.)

JULIA: Ay, what nonsense! If anyone's out there with new school supplies, I haven't seen them.

(There's the sound of distant shooting, men singing.)

(LUCILA goes to the window, looks out.)

LUCILA: I wonder if they're gonna do that all night.

JULIA: Yeah, just what the kids need. A lot of noise keeping them awake—on a school night.

LUCILA: I hear there's a general out there. Little stars all over his chest. He's the one they brought in by helicopter.

JULIA: *(Sarcastic)* Oh, I hear Barrientos himself is going to pay us a visit.

LUCILA: You think so?

JULIA: Please, Lu! It's just a bunch of drunken soldiers acting like fools.

LUCILA: Rosa Ana told me...

(More shouts, gun shots.)

(JULIA goes to the window, shouts.)

JULIA: You guys stop that! I'm telling you! Don't make me go out there!

LUCILA: ...that there are *yanqui* soldiers out there, too.
The ones giving the orders are *yanquis*. And when
they're done torturing him here, they're gonna take
the *Commandante* to Washington D C for more torture.

JULIA: All right, we will now put a moratorium on the
foolish gossip of Rosa Anna.

LUCILA: "Moratorium"? Wait, let me grab my
dictionary, Miss Moratorum.

JULIA: There will be no torture in La Higuera! They
wouldn't dare!

LUCILA: What's wrong with you? You don't realize a lot
of important work is taking place only a few feet from
this house. Instead of being honored, you're agitated.
All day—a bad mood!

JULIA: When generals and helicopters land in your back
yard, Lu, it's time to get a little agitated.

LUCILA: But the men they captured are terrorists, Julia.
Foreign guerillas.

JULIA: I heard the radio. I know what Barrientos wants
us to think.

LUCILA: They say the guerillas do nothing but murder
peasants, steal chickens, and rape women—

JULIA: I never heard they rape women.

LUCILA: Rosa Anna heard it on the radio.

JULIA: Rosa Anna is an ignorant, old gossip who loves
to make things up.

LUCILA: Why are you defending them? They're atheists.
They worship money!

JULIA: Such ignorance! Communists don't worship
money. It's why the *yanquis* hate them so much!

LUCILA: When men are atheists there's nothing they won't do. Men tell the truth only when they think God is listening. God, who knows everything...

JULIA: Don't try to out-God me. I know my God.

LUCILA: ...checking the words men say against the knowledge He has of the Universe. Men don't steal when they know God's watching. They don't blaspheme, cheat on their wives, invade other countries, or rape little girls!

JULIA: Oh now the guerillas are raping little girls.

LUCILA: Look, I know you think I'm an idiot, not a smart-ass like you and Papi—

JULIA: "Idiot" is your word.

LUCILA: But I have two things better than education: faith and instinct. And my instincts are loud—warning me to be careful. To let our leaders do what they think is best and not let our big mouth get us in trouble.

JULIA: I will say whatever I want, whenever I want, to whoever I want. Little stars or no little stars.

LUCILA: I know you. You think all this guerilla activity is so damn romantic.

JULIA: You have no idea what I...

LUCILA: All they are, girl, are dirty, godless foreigners coming here uninvited to spill blood and take our land.

JULIA: So unlike the North Americans—who are good and wise and actually belong in Bolivia!

LUCILA: North Americans believe in God!

JULIA: You never met a North American in your life!

LUCILA: All I can say is when you come across these North Americans—and I know you will, 'cause you never listen to me—you are polite, civil, and you make

them know we are people of great pride and greater
respect.

JULIA: I know how to act in front of strangers.

LUCILA: These are not just strangers. They're strangers
with very big guns.

JULIA: And you wonder why I'm in a bad mood.

(Beat)

LUCILA: I know why you're in a bad mood. You saw
him, didn't you? You saw them bringing him in.

JULIA: I really didn't see him too well...

LUCILA: And by just looking at his face, you think—no,
you know—he's a good man with a good cause and
everything we hear on the radio from our side is crap.
Dear Lord, how did I end up with such a romantic?

JULIA: I saw nothing romantic about the man they
dragged into La Higuera like a dog.

LUCILA: That's not what Rosa Anna said. He's the
most beautiful man she's ever seen.

JULIA: He looked like hell. Not like the pictures.
More like one of those souls who lose their minds
and wander the mountains like an animal.

LUCILA: Like Uncle Joaquin! I still cry!

JULIA: Worse. Uncle Joaquin really did lose his mind.
He didn't understand there's indignity to sleeping in
ditches, peeing in his clothes, walking on all fours,
competing with the dogs for food. His body was in hell
but in his mind he was a little boy, on his mother's lap,
drinking her sweet milk and feasting on her love. No.
The man they captured today wasn't lucky enough to
lose his mind.

LUCILA: Maybe God wants that Communist to learn
something.

JULIA: So the ropes tying his hands are meant to teach him a lesson? Wow! Maybe I'll try that with my kids. Point rifles at them, humiliate them...maybe my kids'll learn so much, they'll be as smart as the geniuses of North America!

LUCILA: Sarcasm is an ugly trait in a woman.

JULIA: Must be why I have so many suitors. *(Beat)* Lu, he looked so scared. He kept looking into the crowd for someone to help him. At one point he looked right at me. I swear, my heart jumped! I thought: this man once had everything, now he has nothing. What's it like to fall so far? Then the soldiers pushed us away from him. *(Beat)* Rosa Anna says they're keeping him in the school.

LUCILA: I thought we were putting a "moratorium" on—

JULIA: If that's true—first thing tomorrow—I'm going to the school to talk to him.

LUCILA: Wait; wait a minute—

JULIA: When Papi was alive if anything important happened in town, it fell on his shoulders. Since he's not here, it falls on me.

LUCILA: But he's a prisoner of the state!

JULIA: In my school! Every person who walks into that ugly, old building is my responsibility.

LUCILA: No, Julia. No. You are to stay away. Do not get mixed up in things you have no—

(LUCILA stops, looks at JULIA—and laughs long and loud.)

JULIA: Now what's wrong with you?

LUCILA: You really think you're gonna find a husband in that school?

JULIA: I swear, words falls out of your mouth and I—

LUCILA: Lonely Julia! No one in La Higuera's good
enough for a snob like you. Now here's a man to make
a girl proud! Famous, handsome and muy macho!

JULIA: I don't fool myself like that, shut up.

LUCILA: A sister knows her sister's heart!

JULIA: I know I'll never have kids of my own except
the dozen boys and girls who go to that school. I'm
resigned to it. *(Beat)* I want to know why he came to this
country. What he thought he was going to accomplish.
What he thinks of our people.

LUCILA: Uh-huh. And you won't be wearing your best
dress, either. Dear Lord, how did I end up with such a
rebel?

JULIA: I thought you said I was a romantic.

LUCILA: The worst kind: a rebellious romantic.
Dying to fuck everything up—

(JULIA laughs, crosses herself.)

JULIA: Sis, your language!

LUCILA: You get in trouble with those soldiers, you're
gonna hear a lot worse. Life isn't hard enough? You're
one of the few women with a job. Someone people look
up to 'cause God gave you brains and dropped some
fire in your heart. We have a decent home and don't
you get it? —One wrong word with the North
Americans and it could all go away, blown apart
like something they hit with a bomb.

JULIA: Good thing they believe in God, huh?

LUCILA: You go to jail, what's gonna happen to me?
Who's gonna take care of me? That awful, stupid Rosa
Anna?

JULIA: I'm not going to jail. I'm going to work. I work
in that school. If there's someone in there, I'm going to

talk to him. Because that's what I do. I don't plant
fields, herd cattle, or make babies. I talk to people.

LUCILA: Yes, you do. God help us all.

(A burst of gunfire draws JULIA *to the window. She looks out
into the uncertain night.)*

(Black out.)

Scene Two

(Morning, October 8, 1967)

*(Outside the one-room school house in La Higuera, a mud-
walled building, white-washed, with a dirt floor and two
small, dirt-covered windows.)*

*(Guarding the entrance to the school are two young Bolivian
Army Rangers, dressed for full combat, holding machine
guns.)*

*(*JULIA *confronts* LIEUTENANT FELIX RODRIGUEZ, *A K A*
FELIX RAMOS, *thirty, a tall, broad-shouldered Cuban
national working for the C I A.)*

(Though it's threadbare and has holes in it, JULIA *is wearing
her nicest dress and earrings. She's put effort into this.)*

(In mid-conversation:)

FELIX: —Miss, I have a horrendous situation here—
completely fucked—and now the fucking Barrientos
gang is breathing down my fucking neck—

*(*JULIA *crosses herself.)*

JULIA: Please don't curse in front of me—

FELIX: —and the fucking North Americans are crawling
up my ASSHOLE. And for all I know, Castro's got
the hills around here filled with commandos and
mercenaries from fucking Bulgaria...

JULIA: First, the noise last night. Unacceptable. You need to discipline each soldier who took part in that orgy of—

(FELIX *looks at his* RANGERS.)

FELIX: Boys, you're in deep shit. Drop and give me twenty.

(*The* RANGERS *grumble quietly to each other and do twenty push-ups.*)

FIRST ARMY RANGER: You believe this shit?

SECOND ARMY RANGER: Cuban asshole.

(FELIX *smiles at* JULIA, *who knows she's being insulted.*)

FELIX: Happy? Move on.

JULIA: And—your prisoner. I need to see him. Right now.

(FELIX *laughs. It just makes* JULIA *angrier.*)

FELIX: Who put you up to this? One of my guys?

JULIA: Sergeant, do you know who I am—?

FELIX: Lieutenant—

JULIA:—do you know who I am in this town? Who my father was? This is my school and I—

FELIX: Well, there's not going to be any school today, I'll tell you that!

JULIA: I know that—but I think you should let me see...

FELIX: That ought to make your kids very happy! I expect to see a lot of smiling little faces in La Higuera today, celebrating a reprieve from the tedium of lessons and homework...

JULIA: Actually my kids are upset by the violence.

FELIX: ...when they ask you who to thank for saving them from the boredom of their school day...

JULIA: "Tedium," "boredom"—nice opinion you have of public education, sir!

FELIX: ...you tell them it was Lieutenant Felix Ramos, liberator, man of the people, who set them free!
(*He laughs.*)

JULIA: If you'd listen you'd know my kids don't feel very free right now—

FELIX: Liberators should be thanked, no? In many nice ways, hot meals, warm place to lay my head after the hot meals...

JULIA: Our school's not religious, but it's always been sacred to us. Here we respect the holiness of the mind. Seeing soldiers with guns around the school...knowing that the man inside is wounded and probably dying...

FELIX: Miss, do you have any idea who I have here? And how dangerous he—?

JULIA: I saw what he looked like when you brought him in. How dangerous can he be?

FELIX: He demolished industries. Ordered the deaths of hundreds of innocent people—by firing squad. Prostituted our culture to the Soviets. And basically killed everything that was beautiful in Cuba.

JULIA: I don't know anything about that. Everyone has a different story about him.

FELIX: For a teacher, you're woefully under-informed.

JULIA: Look, I represent the people of this town. And I must see for myself that no one is being mistreated in this school. It's a matter of the honor of La Higuera!

FELIX: What are you, the mayor or something?

JULIA: People looked up to my father. Now they look up to me.

FELIX: Yes, you are rather tall for a woman.

JULIA: No, you're rather short for a man.

(*The* ARMY RANGERS *laugh.*)

(FELIX *gives them a dirty look, then turns to* JULIA.)

FELIX: We tried twice to interrogate him. He doesn't say a word. What makes you think he'll talk to you?

JULIA: Call it a woman's instinct, sir.

(FELIX's *eyes graze the pretty school teacher with not-so-subtle sexual appreciation.*)

FELIX: All his life he's been a magnet for women like you.

JULIA: What is a "woman like" me?

FELIX: ...from spoiled, rich bitches, to naive, revolutionary whores who fell under his spell. I guess it's happening even here, in this fucking pig-sty.

JULIA: Don't insult my intelligence. Or my intentions. Or my community. In my eyes you're no better than he is—another interfering foreigner.

FELIX: If you were my wife, I'd slap you across the face.

(*Unafraid of* FELIX, JULIA *doesn't flinch.*)

JULIA: Then fate's been kind to the both of us. Do I go in with your permission or without it?

(FELIX *glances at the two* RANGERS, *amazed, impressed. The men smirk at each other, appreciating her passionate nature.*)

FELIX: These country girls are something else, huh? Give birth in the morning and plow a man's field that very night!

(FELIX *looks her over again. Maybe there's a way he can use her...*)

Tell you what, Miss. I like your balls. You don't look like a terrorist. And I'm a generous man. I'll give you a half hour with him...but only if I'm in there with you—

JULIA: Alone.

FELIX: How can I leave you in there alone?

JULIA: Do you think he's going to feel free to talk if you're next to me? *(Beat)* Look—I just want to talk to him—about nothing—the stupid weather—nothing political or subversive. I promise we are not going to plot the overthrow of Barrientos. *(Beat)* I just think, well, a man as secure and powerful as you...would think it's merciful to let him have some human—

FELIX: Merciful. A word he barely fucking knows. Miss, do you think anything in life is free?

JULIA: The things that God...

FELIX: Nothing is free. You want to go in. I want information. If I let you in, alone, then I need something in return. Now, don't say yes just to shut me up. These men've been planning violent revolution in Bolivia. That means your people die. Your students suffer. If you love your country, if you have any patriotism in the heart beating in that pretty, little chest...you'll tell me what you learn in there.

JULIA: You're not even Bolivian, what do you care? Are you Colombian? Panamanian? Don't be ashamed, tell me.

FELIX: Cuban—and I'm not ashamed—

JULIA: God, you're Cuban? The poor guy doesn't have a chance, does he?

FELIX: It's a lot more fucked up than you know, Miss. You've no idea what I'm trying to do for him. If it was up to these Bolivian animals, he'd be dead already!

JULIA: If you want to do something for him, let me show him not all Bolivians are animals. For just an hour, please.

FELIX: The information I asked for?

JULIA: Look, if I learn anything really important, I'll tell you.

FELIX: On your honor?

JULIA: On my honor. But you know he's not going to tell me anything you don't already know.

FELIX: He might surprise us. He does that a lot.

(Beat. JULIA *studies him.)*

JULIA: You admire him, don't you?

FELIX: He raped my country. Stole my government. And delivered my beloved nation to the Communists and atheists. What do you think?

*(*JULIA *has no response: fixes* FELIX *with her intense glare.)*

*(*FELIX *delivers this as much for his men as for her:)*

You may have a half hour with the prisoner. Then you're to report back to me for de-briefing.

(A small, mocking smile on JULIA's *face.)*

JULIA: Yes, sir, Sergeant!

FELIX: My men and I will be outside at all times. Under no circumstances are you to touch the prisoner. Spread your arms and legs, please.

JULIA: Excuse me?

FELIX: I said spread your fucking arms and legs. Please.

*(*JULIA *stands with her legs spread and puts her arms up.)*

*(*FELIX *motions to the two* ARMY RANGERS, *who pat* JULIA *down. They touch her inappropriately, try not to laugh.)*

*(FELIX pats her down for good measure. JULIA, maintaining
her dignity, trying not to shake, doesn't look him in the eye.)*

JULIA: Find what you're looking for in there?

FELIX: Inside.

*(The FIRST ARMY RANGER opens the door to the
schoolhouse.)*

*(FELIX suddenly, violently grabs JULIA by the hair,
pulls her head back. Tight whisper:)*

FELIX: And don't you ever fucking mock me again,
bitch.

(Black out)

END OF ACT ONE

ACT TWO

(FELIX *and the two* ARMY RANGERS *lead* JULIA *into the dank, dark little school room.*)

(*There are a couple of small wooden desks along the wall. A rough wooden table serves as the teacher's desk. An old slate blackboard against the wall with Spanish verbs, written in chalk, being conjugated.*)

(*The room is so impoverished it seems more suited to farm animals than to children.*)

(*Lying in a small pool of blood on the dirt floor, his bleeding legs tied together, and his arms tied behind his back, is* ERNESTO "CHE" GUEVARA, *an Argentine of thirty-nine.*)

(CHE *is emaciated, his thick black hair is long, matted, tangled, and his dark beard is long and wild. His clothes are tattered, his shoes are rags wrapped around bloody feet. He stinks like an animal.*)

(CHE *is exhausted, hungry, thirsty, in extreme pain.*)

(*Yet, there is a defiance and energy and fearlessness in his eyes that make his visitors pause at the doorway.*)

(*The* ARMY RANGERS *look at him with almost supernatural fear.* FELIX *is, as* JULIA *said, admiring, respectful and conflicted.*)

(*Only* JULIA *seems to take him in as what he is—a brave, broken man pushed to his physical and emotional limit.*)

(CHE *looks at the four of them with undisguised contempt—
though the sight of the young woman softens his glare.
He has no idea why his captors have brought her here.*)

(*After a moment in which no one speaks or moves,*
FELIX *turns to the* ARMY RANGERS.)

FELIX: Outside.

(*The* ARMY RANGERS *glance at* CHE, *then turn to leave.
The* FIRST ARMY RANGER *whispers to the* SECOND ARMY
RANGER.)

FIRST ARMY RANGER: You think they're gonna fuck?

(*The* SECOND ARMY RANGER *laughs.*)

SECOND ARMY RANGER: I fuckin' hope so!

(*The* ARMY RANGERS *are gone.*)

(FELIX *stares at* CHE.)

FELIX: Did you sleep well, *Commandante*?

(CHE *doesn't answer. Stares at them relentlessly.*)

(*Disgusted by what she sees,* JULIA *shakes her head.*)

JULIA: God, forgive the things we do to each other...

FELIX: I get the impression the *Commandante*'s a bit
depressed this morning. Why do you think I'd get
that impression?

(CHE *doesn't answer. Stares silently*)

JULIA: Did you give him anything to eat?

(FELIX *ignores her.*)

FELIX: You're wondering what happened to your pal,
Willi. He's still alive, in case you give a shit.

(CHE *doesn't answer. Looks away, sick of staring at them.*)

(FELIX *gets closer to* CHE, *squats close to the ground.*)

Look. I know you think we're pigs. And you have the
right to invade a sovereign country and kill people and
rape girls because you—

(At the word "rape" CHE *spits at* FELIX.*)*

CHE: Liar!

FELIX: —because you have—what?—some strange new
form of moral superiority? I'm letting this woman...

JULIA: My name's Julia, sir.

FELIX: ...talk to you, alone, for a few moments, not
because I've got some hidden agenda or I'm trying
to get information or convert you to the joys of
capitalism...but because it's the, you know, humane
thing to do and we're not all a bunch of filthy, hopeless
barbarians.

*(*CHE *doesn't answer. Adjusts his position to make himself
more comfortable, but the pain is intense no matter what he
does—but he never cries out.)*

*(*FELIX *goes to* JULIA.*)*

FELIX: I'll be outside if he threatens to hurt you in any
way. As much as it pains these subversives to know
this, no harm can come to you as long as you're under
the care and protection of the Bolivian Armed Forces.
Isn't that right, my Julia?

*(*JULIA *stares at* FELIX *as if he were speaking Martian.)*

*(*FELIX *suddenly reaches out to touch her cheek.)*

*(*JULIA *pulls back, startled.)*

FELIX: Good.

*(*FELIX *glances, a bit nervous, at* CHE, *then leaves the room.)*

*(*JULIA *and* CHE *are alone.)*

*(She looks at him, sadly taking in the sight of his wounds,
his deplorable condition.)*

(CHE *doesn't look at* JULIA; *he barely moves. The only sound is his subtle wheezing as his asthma kicks in. Never becoming a full-out asthma attack, his bad breathing is a constant presence.*)

(JULIA *steps a little closer to* CHE.)

JULIA: Next time, I'll see if I can bring water and food. I can't believe they just threw you in here...

(*She trails off, inhibited by* CHE's *stubborn silence, his seething anger.*)

JULIA: I won't stay if you don't want me to. I don't work for them. I'm from here, La Higuera—all my life—and I just needed to see what was—

CHE: What are you doing here?

JULIA: I was—when they brought you in last night, I—

CHE: Are you here with the same curiosity a child feels when she's visiting the zoo?

JULIA: Yes, I was curious, but I'm not a child and I won't be spoken to like one.

CHE: You satisfied your curiosity.

JULIA: Look, sir, I just wanted to talk to you—

CHE: That would require my listening. Why the hell should I listen to you?

JULIA: No reason. But I thought you might like, I don't know, someone...I mean, I can't imagine how awful—

CHE: I abhor pity.

JULIA: I don't pity you—

CHE: Take it outside and shower it on your country, Miss. Pity the poor of Bolivia: the young men drafted into a fascist military, taking orders from foreigners and—

JULIA: Sir, I care about my country and my people. You shouldn't question that—

CHE: By the way you dress, I see your station in life is quite a bit higher than the average person of this town. How much pity can you show these people when you look down on them from—?

JULIA: I don't look down on anyone! Who do you think you are, judging me? You haven't looked at my face! How can you know who you're talking to?

CHE: If the amorous Lieutenant Ramos brings you to me, what else am I to think—?

JULIA: Amorous? I practically had to force my way into this school. And this is my school! Every sad, suffering inch of it! Mine, you darn idiot!

(For the first time, CHE turns his eyes to JULIA. His look is sharp, penetrating, merciless.)

CHE: What did you call me?

JULIA: Oh my God: I'm sorry. I can't believe— my sister's right—my big mouth—

CHE: What did you promise the Lieutenant?

(Beat)

JULIA: Any information I get from you.

CHE: You're honest at least. And you have a temper. I can respect that.

JULIA: Not everyone likes a woman who speaks her mind.

CHE: I didn't say I liked it. *(Beat)* How is this pigsty your school?

JULIA: I. I'm the teacher here. I've been teaching since I was nineteen. My father and I used to teach under a tree. We built this school together five years ago.

*(CHE studies her a long moment...trying to remain strong
and aloof, yet secretly seeking some connection.)*

CHE: Willi, my companion-in-arms, was a teacher.
The only one of my men taken alive. Do you know
where they're keeping him?

*(JULIA is relieved they've momentarily moved beyond
hostility...)*

JULIA: I don't.

CHE: Every time we captured a wounded enemy
soldier, I treated their wounds. They're not going
to treat Willi's wounds. They're going to let him sit
in his own blood.

JULIA: We don't know. It's in God's hands now.

CHE: Is that what you teach your students? The rank
fatalism of the Church? Dead myths and fairy tales
about some creature called God?

(JULIA almost recoils—deeply offended.)

JULIA: God isn't a fairy tale, sir. God is—God is God!

(CHE almost laughs at her.)

CHE: Yes, God is God.

*(Silence between them—a mini-crossroads. Do they continue
in hostility or find another path?)*

(JULIA starts to leave.)

JULIA: Look, I'll go...

(JULIA is at the door when she hears—)

CHE: How many students do you have? Miss—?

(JULIA stops.)

JULIA: Cortes. *(She turns to look at him.)* Julia. It depends.

(CHE's cold look demands that she continue.)

JULIA: Uhm, it's never the same from day to day...it depends on the work they have to do for their families, or if someone in the family's sick—

CHE: In Cuba this wouldn't be called a school. It's disgraceful. I can't believe it's only five years old. It has the smell of shit in it. This building would be called a prison in Cuba.

JULIA: Yes, it's a poor school—we never put down a floor and I don't keep it clean the way I should— but I do what I can to give my kids some minimal—

(CHE *indicates the blackboard.*)

CHE: Do you know you made a mistake in grammar?

(JULIA *looks at the blackboard.*)

JULIA: What are you talking about?

CHE: Right there. You conjugated the imperative form of "*huir*". You wrote "*tu huyes, el huya, nosotros huyamos, ellos huyan*".

JULIA: Yeah, that's right.

CHE: You left out "*vosotros huid!*"

JULIA: Normal people don't say "*vosotros huid!*"

CHE: They most certainly do! They say it in Argentina!

JULIA: We're not in Argentina, are we?

CHE: And it's a good thing because in Argentina they probably wouldn't grant you a teaching license!

JULIA: Well, excuse me, but in some places on earth you don't need a license to teach.

CHE: And that's a very useful excuse for incompetence!

JULIA: You don't know what you're talking about!

CHE: Do you teach your children why they're poor?

(JULIA *pauses, the question has thrown her.*)

JULIA: They're poor because their parents are poor.

CHE: They're poor because they're in a system that keeps them poor. And you're part of that system!

JULIA: Are you saying I keep my children poor?

CHE: If you don't teach them how their lives are manipulated by the *yanqui* imperialists, if all you do is apologize for the crimes of your government—

JULIA: I don't have time to teach them about systems. I teach them how not to die every day.

CHE: Even when it's the system itself that's killing them?

(JULIA *takes a breath in order not to lose her temper.*)

JULIA: That's all fine rhetoric, sir—but it's not the reality here. *(Beat)* My father gave me, and La Higuera, everything he had. And with almost no help from the government or the church, we built this "prison" as you like to call it, using his life savings, so our kids wouldn't go around thinking—I don't know—the world is flat or sickness comes from witchcraft—or not know there are actual numbers bigger than "three." Of course some days I have to contend with the machete-waving grandfather who thinks I'm teaching the children to be too independent. Or the irate mother who thinks I'm teaching their daughters to write love letters to their secret boyfriends. Or the over-protective brother who wants to strangle me for using the word "sex" in class. And whether I like it or not, I come to work anyway—though I haven't been paid by the "system" in a year and a half. God! It'd be so much easier, trust me, to throw my hands up in despair and leave their education to nature, or chance, or to the insane, old *brujas* of the town! *(Beat)* Most days I'm lucky to have five kids in here. The rest are out there trying not to starve to death. Yet through storms, head lice, or crazy parents—I'm here every day for those five kids, sir, no questions asked, oh, unless I'm attending one of their funerals. Which I seem to be doing more and more these days.

(Short silence)

(CHE looks at her, feeling a flicker of respect for her obvious intelligence and strength.)

CHE: Of course it can't be easy teaching under these circumstances.

JULIA: Look, I know who you are. I know you spoke to the United Nations and had dinner with Mao Tse Tung...

CHE: Actually, we just talked; Mao had a cold and wasn't very hungry that—

JULIA: I know you don't need me to tell you anything. But it seems...it's you—not me—who's looking down on these people. What happened? Did you come to Bolivia and expect my poor neighbors to bow down to you because you're the great Che Guevara? Huh? Didn't work out that way, did it?

CHE: What gave it away? The bullet wounds in my legs?

(Silence)

(CHE looks at JULIA a long moment, impossible to tell what he's thinking.)

(JULIA looks away, afraid she's offended him irrevocably.)

JULIA: God, I'm sorry. I came because I wanted to, I don't know, to help you in some way, I guess...

CHE: Miss Cortes...

JULIA: ...But I'm not doing a very good job. Maybe you're right: I'm just a mediocre teacher— no, you said incompetent. That's nicer, thanks.

CHE: I didn't mean to insult you.

JULIA: So I should go and leave you in God's hands—
in the hands of the Great Myth. I hope He's merciful—

CHE: Please don't leave me in God's hands!

JULIA: I'm sorry, but if I can't do good, I don't want to
be here—

(JULIA *starts to leave.*)

CHE: Miss Cortes, I'm ordering you to stay!

(JULIA *continues for the door, shaking her head.*)

CHE: That is, I'm asking you to stay!

(JULIA *stops.*)

CHE: Please, Miss.

(JULIA *looks at him.*)

JULIA: I just—I have such...I know it's not much, but
I love my country. And I don't want to see anyone get
hurt. But they say you invaded Bolivia to—

CHE: Bolivia is an illusion. A fiction. That's the first
thing you have to understand, Julia.

(JULIA *almost startles to hear him say her name—she tries to
cover her surprise.*)

JULIA: I'm sorry—what?

CHE: Bolivia is an arbitrary name given to arbitrary
lines on some fat bureaucrat's corrupted map.
And such stability! Two hundred governments
since 1825—one every nine months!

JULIA: I know my history, sad as it is.

CHE: The point is, we're all part of the same *mestizo*
race. And except for the indigenous, we all speak the
same language...well, most of us...

(JULIA *can't prevent an ironic smile.*)

JULIA: Yes, most of us. (*She goes to the blackboard, writes and says:*) "*Vosotros huid.*"

CHE: Yet, despite our shared history, we're told we're separate and distinct nations. Why? Who does this benefit? Do you think we do? We are isolated by these borders. Weakened. And the weaknesses of the plundered people of this continent are exploited by capitalist thugs in a sick, imperialist dream to homogenize the world—to sell each country, piece by piece, to the U S monopolies. In the world-wide revolutionary struggle against colonial bondage there are no borders, Julia! In the socialist transformation of humanity itself, Bolivia is Vietnam! Vietnam is Bolivia...why are you smiling at me like an idiot?

JULIA: I know you're passionate about this, Mister Guevara...but you really need to learn to talk to people like a person...not like a speech you give at the Kremlin.

(*There's the barest hint of a smile on* CHE's *lips.*)

CHE: Don't call me Mister Guevara. It pisses me off.

JULIA: Well, that's a lot better.

CHE: See? Even an old war-horse can learn a few things.

JULIA: See? I'm not such a bad teacher, am I?

CHE: No. You're not. Your children are lucky to have you.

JULIA: You should tell them.

CHE: I doubt I'll ever get the chance.

(*Beat*)

JULIA: We don't know what's going to happen. Nobody knows but God. And God's plan is invisible to us. Just have some faith...

CHE: Faith is trash. Faith is excrement. I'd rather have a pistol and some fucking ammunition.

(JULIA *crosses herself.*)

JULIA: I know God is great enough not to take offense at that.

CHE: What God should take offense at is the condition of the people here. Julia, you can't tell me it doesn't affect you. Fifty years ago half the indigenous children in Bolivia died before the age of two. Today, it's no better: the people live almost like savages here— in a state of poverty that breaks your heart. Entire families live and sleep and cook in one miserable room. They have no clothes. No water. Nothing.

JULIA: I have eyes; I can see it....

CHE: Forgive me—you mention God—there is no God evil enough to allow these injustices to go unchallenged. Where is God? Is He asleep? Has the Old Fart finally died?

JULIA: For the love of God, please don't say things like that in front of me.

CHE: I just don't understand how you can sleep at night knowing...

JULIA: Well, what about Cuba? Isn't Cuba poor? Why didn't you stay there? Why don't you help them?

CHE: Cuba is very poor. But in Cuba you have one thing you don't find here, even among the poorest of the poor. And that's hope.

JULIA: Is there real hope or is it just an illusion?

CHE: Even the illusion of hope is better than despair. And that's what I see in your country—despair I've never experienced in Cuba after the revolution. You can't tell me, when you look in your children's eyes, that you don't see it.

(Beat)

JULIA: I see some amazing things when I look in their eyes. *(Beat)* Are you married? Do you have a family?

CHE: I have a wife in Cuba. Aleida. We have four— Aliusha, Celia, Ernesto and Camilo. My ex-wife is Hilda. Our daughter is Hildita.

JULIA: What's she like, Aleida?

(CHE hesitates—unsure.)

CHE: She loves the movies. She loves to dance. She loves green things. And.

(CHE hesitates again—but is unable to keep the memory from coming...)

Last year, when I returned to Cuba from the Congo, no one was supposed to know I was back—no one but Fidel, Aleida, and a few in the government. But I was desperate to see my children before I left for Bolivia. I went home in my disguise...the hairs on my head were pulled out one by one until I was bald...I wore thick glasses...and I pretended to be their "Uncle Ramon". The hardest thing I ever had to do—say good-bye to my children without letting them know it was me. When I hugged Aliusha tight, she went running back to Aleida and said, "I think that old man's in love with me!" It was everything I could do to keep from—well— I don't know how Aleida controlled herself. That's the kind of woman she is.

(JULIA and CHE are both surprised that he's revealed so much, so quickly.)

JULIA: Do you miss her?

CHE: Don't ask me stupid questions.

JULIA: Yet you're here, a million miles from home—

CHE: Fighting for my ideals. So my children's world will be more just, more humane.

JULIA: You don't think they'd rather have you at their side? That your presence would make their world better?

CHE: They understand why I'm here and they approve. That's all I have to say about it.

JULIA: I know I'd rather have my father with me than to know he died for his ideals...

CHE: Have I died already? I thought I was still alive.

JULIA: Of course you are—

CHE: Unless you know something I don't—

JULIA: No, I'm sorry—

CHE: Do you know what Ramos plans to do with me?

JULIA: No—I just—I think of those idiots out there—

CHE: What about you? Are you married? Where's your family?

JULIA: My family is my sister and me. She's sick. Most foods disagree with her. And there are so many shortages here, she's malnourished. I take care of her. There's no one else. No husband, no man.

CHE: You're still young and very...well, not all that un-attractive...there's no reason for you to be alone.

JULIA: Yes, well, my work doesn't leave a lot of room for romance. No matter what my sister thinks. She's always making fun of me for being: (Imitates LUCILA) "A pathetic, romantic fool."

CHE: Imagine that.

JULIA: This is a world where life can get so small and simple. Men raise pigs and grow kinoa and potatoes. There's birth and death and the little, unimportant things that happen in between.

CHE: Yet those "little things" are everything, don't you think?

(JULIA *can't help but laugh.*)

JULIA: You're a hypocrite, you know that?

CHE: Are you actually laughing at me?

JULIA: Those "little things," Che...I mean, Mister—

CHE: Che. It's Che. Actually it's *el* Che, but you can drop the "*el*" if you wish.

JULIA: Weren't they the things you had before you came here? A wife, her smile, her words, your children's voices in the morning...you had them, they were yours. But they weren't enough for you. You wanted...

CHE: To change everything and everyone around me.

JULIA: Yes, the whole crazy world. *(Beat)* I'm sorry. I don't mean to criticize you.

CHE: I can take criticism.

JULIA: I'm sure you can, but I'm in no position to judge you.

CHE: Leaders must be judged.

JULIA: I guess I don't understand you, and, I don't know, I guess if it was me and I had your life, I would've been happy and I would've stayed home to savor all the good things that were coming to me, the things I earned from my hard work.

CHE: Such as?

JULIA: My children's love. A love that can change the world—

CHE: "A love that can change the world"! That's brilliant!

JULIA:—the devotion and trust of my spouse. The years
as they add up on my children's faces. The world
reflected in their eyes. A family that's like a coat you
spread around your body and nothing can harm you.
Not disease or sadness or old age. Someone to say your
name in a voice no one else in the world uses.

CHE: Yes, you must drive your sister absolutely crazy.

JULIA: It would be nice if you would take what I say
seriously.

CHE: I bet you've been thinking this romantic nonsense
all your life.

JULIA: Yes, well, La Higuera can be a lonely place.

CHE: Yet you've never left.

JULIA: I didn't see a reason.

CHE: Funny. I've done nothing but leave.

JULIA: You're a man, you're allowed.

CHE: Bullshit. You could've left. In Cuba, many women
besides Aleida left the safety of their homes to fight in
the Sierra Maestra.

JULIA: The world isn't Cuba.

CHE: Well, it should be. And someday it will be. And
schools like this won't exist. Every place will have new
modern schools, with actual floors, and large windows,
and the latest textbooks, and not just one sorry,
burned-out teacher who can't conjugate—

JULIA: I can too!

CHE: —but an army of dedicated teachers, working
around the clock—and not only will they educate the
children, they will educate the family. It's pointless
to bring a child to school only to send them home to
ignorance and superstition. Learning must happen
every minute. Mothers and fathers must be educated

and must be able to teach each other, their children,
and every child in the village. Can you imagine?
A world of constant learning...every person will
simultaneously be teacher and student...

(CHE *stops—a stabbing pain in his stomach doubles him
over. Though he does his best not to cry out, the pain is too
great to keep inside.*)

(CHE *coughs, spits up blood.*)

(JULIA *watches, alarmed, unable to help him, torn between
wanting to go to him and calling out for help.*)

(CHE's *intense pain continues through the scene...*)

JULIA: I can't believe they let you lie here without—

CHE: I'm alright—it'll pass—

JULIA: I can call the Lieutenant—

CHE: I'd rather vomit my lungs!

JULIA: It's disgusting what they're doing to you.
I can't believe my own government would let—

CHE: If your government allows such poverty and
misery, why are you surprised they'd treat a combatant
like this?

JULIA: We're supposed to be a God-fearing, Christian
nation—

CHE: It's been my experience the more a country
invokes the name of God the more likely they are to
torture and destroy their own and other people. You
can't be naive about the intentions of your government.
Especially since you don't really have a government.

JULIA: Are you sure you're okay...?

(CHE *doesn't want to surrender to the terrible pain.*)

CHE: Your government has a government. Did you
know that? And it's this greater government which

really controls what happens in this school. Who do you think your friend Lieutenant Ramos works for?

(JULIA *is still pre-occupied with his pain.*)

JULIA: Please don't call him my friend.

CHE: North Americans train the specialists and mercenaries who hunted me down. North Americans pay Ramos to interrogate me and photograph my journal and torture my companions. North Americans shove money up the ass of your President Barrientos and force the right words to come out of his mouth.

(JULIA *looks at* CHE—*a little shocked over his last metaphor.*)

(CHE *can see his language has offended her.*)

CHE: Now what is it?

JULIA: I'm sorry—I don't like—I know you're a soldier—

CHE: My language.

JULIA: Yes, your language. I'm sorry—I—

CHE: The North Americans fuck Barrientos up the ass in order to make the cocksucker do their bidding. That language?

JULIA: Oh God—that's really bad—

(JULIA *crosses herself.*)

CHE: Don't do that.

JULIA: Do what?

CHE: Cross yourself.

JULIA: Why not?

CHE: It's inane. It does nothing but make you look like an ignorant ape.

JULIA: I'm sorry—but I will cross myself as often as I need to—

CHE: To ward off the evil of evil language?

JULIA: Because it puts me closer to God—

CHE: ASS—!

(JULIA *crosses herself.*)

JULIA: Stop it.

CHE: FUCKING THE ASS—!

(JULIA *crosses herself.*)

JULIA: Oh God!

CHE: BIG FAT, GROSS TITS COVERED IN THE SEMEN OF THE LOCAL PRIEST!

(JULIA *crosses herself.*)

JULIA: My God, I can't believe this! You're going to burn in hell for this!

(CHE *tries not to laugh.*)

(JULIA *laughs despite herself and crosses herself again.*)

CHE: Really? For how long?

JULIA: Eternity!

CHE: Not long enough! Lyndon Johnson likes to fuck the Pope up his holy butt-hole with a twelve inch crucifix—!

JULIA: Enough! Enough! Please!

(JULIA *stands, laughing, unable to look at him.*)

(CHE *laughs—a loud, sweet, energized laugh: a sound we'd never expect from a body so wracked.*)

(*The door opens.* FELIX *comes in, his gun drawn.*)

(FELIX *sees* JULIA *in the corner, laughing. Then looks over at* CHE, *lying on the ground, laughing.* FELIX *shakes his head, suspicious and slightly annoyed.*)

(JULIA *and* CHE *try to stifle their laughter—but it only makes it worse.*)

FELIX: Party ends in two minutes.

(FELIX *closes the door.*)

(JULIA *and* CHE *stop laughing and look at each other— a new bond between them.*)

(*Then* CHE's *expression is suddenly serious.*)

CHE: Ignorance.

(*No response from* JULIA, *who doesn't understand why he said that.*)

CHE: Repression of speech. Exploitation of children. Economic slavery. Structural injustice. Torture, rape, poverty. I'm disappointed, Julia. These are some of the dirtiest words in the language, yet you don't...

(JULIA *slowly crosses herself.*)

JULIA: I guess I'm an "ignorant ape."

CHE: If my hand was free, I'd be doing the same thing.

JULIA: I'm sorry I got so stupid about your language— like a damn six-year-old.

CHE: You need to get out of the house more often.

JULIA: I do. I haven't laughed like that in...

CHE: I haven't had this kind of contact in the whole, awful year I've been in Bolivia. To talk to someone about something other than the endless guerilla war against the infinite enemy. To simply talk to another human being.

JULIA: It is a strange joy, to be listened to.

CHE: To be listened to. (*Beat*) I don't know what's going to happen. My army is decimated. I have no way to

communicate with the outside world. These barbarians
could torture me until I die—

JULIA: I wouldn't let that happen. I swear to God,
I won't let them touch you.

CHE: I appreciate your—

JULIA: Look in my eyes. I know you laugh at my faith.
But God tells me to never allow another man or woman
to suffer if I can stop it. I will prevent it, I promise you.

CHE: I believe you believe what you're saying. What
I'm trying to say...it's clumsy, I know...is that I won't
forget our conversation. I'll never forget your name.
And that you came to be with me today, when
everyone else, it seems, has disappeared. Forgotten.
Loneliness is a curse. It can break you down faster than
starvation itself. It fills your world with fear. You're
lucky—you're never alone because you have, for want
of a better word— "God".

JULIA: Now, was it really that hard to say?

CHE: Yes, it was, actually. You have—that. And you'll
never be alone. And me? I have you. Today and
tomorrow, no matter what happens, I have God
because I have...

*(The door opens. FELIX comes in with the two ARMY
RANGERS. FELIX barely looks at JULIA.)*

FELIX: You're finished.

*(Not sure what to do, JULIA is motionless, until one of the
ARMY RANGERS shoves her toward the door.)*

CHE: Ramos!

JULIA: What's going on?

CHE: Careful how you handle her! I will not tolerate it!

FELIX: Oh you won't? What the fuck are you going to
do about it?

JULIA: What are you going to do?

FELIX: Take her out.

(The FIRST ARMY RANGER *grabs* JULIA*'s arms and pulls her out the door.)*

FELIX: I honestly don't know another man alive—
though he's tied up, beaten in battle, held prisoner
and reeking of fear—can still make two sovereign
nations shit their pants. You're a marvel, Mister
Guevara. *(To* SECOND ARMY RANGER*)* Help me, moron!

(The SECOND ARMY RANGER *helps* FELIX *lift* CHE *to his feet.)*

*(*CHE*'s body is an open wound and his willpower is concentrated on not letting them see how much pain he's in.)*

FELIX: Cables and radio communiques are flying
between La Paz and Washington D C because of you.
Here's a secret: President Rene Barrientos is not your
buddy.

CHE: Barrientos is as illegitimate as you are.

FELIX: He was elected by the people!

CHE: After he came to power in a coup! Such noble
friends, Ramos!

FELIX: Well, my noble friend wants us to cut off
your dick, shove it in your mouth, cut your head off,
and send the whole sweet package to Castro for his
birthday. That's a direct quote. The United States—

CHE: Your fucking employer—

FELIX: The United States, my fucking employer,
would like to keep you alive long enough to ship you to
Panama for interrogation. There's a U S helicopter a few
miles from here ready to take you to a battleship off the
coast of Chile. Nobody can seem to agree on what to do
with you right now. Frankly, if it was up to me, I'd

drown you in a lake of shit. Alas, I don't get what I want. So until these morons can figure out what to do with you, you're going to live at least another day. More than I can say for your pal Willi, by-the-way. He died, alone, ten minutes ago while you were having fun with your girlfriend. Don't be sad—it's time to smile for posterity.

(FELIX *and the* SECOND ARMY RANGER *drag* CHE *to the door—his wounded leg makes him unable to walk or stand for very long.*)

(*Outside the school,* JULIA *stands with* LUCILA. *They hold each other as* FELIX *brings* CHE *into the sunlight.*)

(LUCILA, *getting her first look at* CHE, *gasps, crosses herself.*)

(CHE *squints, not used to the brightness. He looks around until he spots* JULIA. *He calls to her—*)

CHE: Julia. Come closer.

(JULIA *steps toward* CHE, *but the* FIRST ARMY RANGER *roughly blocks her way.*)

(*The* SECOND ARMY RANGER *has a camera.*)

(FELIX *stands with* CHE—*rigid, enraged, humiliated— as the* SECOND ARMY RANGER *gets his picture.*)

(*A bright flash*)

(*Black out*)

END OF ACT TWO

ACT THREE

(The next afternoon, October 9, 1967)

(Inside the school house)

*(CHE lies on his side, asleep. Arms still tied together.
The pants leg over his wound is now caked in dried blood,
pus, and mud. His hair is still wild and tangled.)*

(The door opens.)

(FELIX enters. Looks at the sleeping CHE.)

(Behind him, holding a pot of hot soup, is JULIA.)

(They both look at the sleeping CHE.)

JULIA: What's going to happen?

FELIX: It's out of my hands.

JULIA: I know you're a soldier and soldiers follow
orders, but don't you have any say...?

FELIX: You goddamn peasants don't understand shit.
My boss tore me a new asshole for what happened
yesterday—you don't understand the risks I'm taking
with you. And I'm doing these things for you without
asking anything in return. And I could ask for a lot.

JULIA: If you want to, you can take whatever you want.
Without asking.

FELIX: I have that power.

JULIA: Power over a powerless, peasant schoolteacher,
but no power over him.

FELIX: It's the way the cards were dealt. Ten minutes.

JULIA: Then?

FELIX: I stand by the radio day and night waiting for an answer to that question.

(FELIX *goes to* CHE *and kicks him lightly on the backside.*)

FELIX: Guevara!

(CHE *stirs. In terrible pain. Sits up and looks at* FELIX, *silent and apprehensive—then at* JULIA.)

(*Now that* CHE's *awake,* FELIX *seems more nervous than usual. He turns to* JULIA.)

FELIX: Last time. (*He leaves.*)

(JULIA *stands at the door, holds the soup, nervous.*)

(*Though still in pain,* CHE *is greatly relieved to see* JULIA.)

JULIA: My sister thought...

CHE: I'm glad you came back.

JULIA: ...you'd like some chicken soup. God knows the good Lieutenant isn't going to feed you—

CHE: Did you sleep well?

JULIA: Uhm—no—are you hungry?

CHE: I'm sorry—it's the second day in a row that I've kept you from teaching school.

JULIA: Believe me, I don't mind, and for most of my kids, you're a hero.

CHE: Smells so good.

JULIA: I killed the chicken myself. Twisted its neck with my own two hands.

CHE: Nothing like a little home cooking.

(JULIA *approaches* CHE, *kneels at his side, holding the soup.*)

(CHE *can't wait—he's nearly salivating.*)

(*But first,* JULIA *puts the pot of soup on the ground and folds her hands in prayer.*)

CHE: What the hell are you doing?

JULIA: Dear God, the food you put in our bodies is one of your truest miracles. Please give us, today and always, the intelligence, grace and civilized humility to be thankful for it. Amen.

(JULIA *looks at* CHE, *waiting.*)

CHE: What?

JULIA: Amen.

CHE: Fucking Christ alive! Amen!

JULIA: Thank you.

(JULIA *picks up the soup, brings the steaming pot close to* CHE's *face. She looks in his eyes.*)

(*And spoons the hot soup into* CHE's *mouth.*)

(*Connected by the food,* JULIA *and* CHE *are both aware of the fragile, but real, intimacy of this gesture.*)

(*The soup is the first real food* CHE's *enjoyed in a year. It does, indeed, taste like a small miracle.*)

CHE: Oooh...God, God, God...!

JULIA: Do you like it?

(*She continues to spoon-feed him through the following.*)

CHE: This—oh, for this alone, you deserve—

JULIA: Shut up and enjoy.

(CHE *eats more soup in silence.*)

(JULIA *enjoys how he's enjoying it.*)

CHE: I'm surprised they let you come back.

JULIA: I came to the school this morning all prepared for an argument with the Lieutenant. But he was—strangely passive with me....

CHE: What's happening out there?

JULIA: It's real quiet. The helicopter that brought the Lieutenant is just sitting there, waiting. It's like all of my neighbors are in hiding. People aren't speaking.

CHE: Soldiers?

JULIA: Same number as yesterday, as far as I can tell.

CHE: Journalists?

JULIA: I don't think so. I don't think anyone knows about this but us.

(CHE *ponders this a moment and what it implies.*)

CHE: Have they brought in any more of my men?

JULIA: I haven't heard anything.

CHE: Anything about what they might do with me?

JULIA: Nothing.

CHE: If there's any way you can find that out for me...

JULIA: I'll try; I will. *(Beat)* Did you dream?

CHE: I dreamed about Cuba.

JULIA: Really? That's what the Lieutenant told me. Last night he dreamed about Cuba.

CHE: Different Cuba. *(Beat)* I was flying over Cuba. There were cold hands on me. The sun was bright but I couldn't close my eyes. Many strange voices. But I couldn't really hear them.

JULIA: He told me he dreamed about the two of you, walking together on the beach, having a pleasant conversation, like brothers!

CHE: I don't think I like him talking to you so much.

JULIA: Really? Why not?

CHE: It's not important, Miss.

(Beat)

JULIA: I was thinking this morning how much you would've liked my father. *(Beat)* He was the tallest man in the province. Taught himself to read. The unelected mayor of La Higuera. The man with all the answers! He could mesmerize a plaza full of people. Never turned down a beggar or turned away a child who wanted to learn. My sister was never happy I decided to follow in his footsteps and teach school. She blames my profession for the fact that I never married. Which is true, I'm afraid. *(Beat)* And the fact that my father spoiled me a little, when it comes to what a man should be.

(JULIA scoops up the last of the soup and gently puts the spoon in CHE's mouth.)

(JULIA and CHE make long eye contact in silence as he swallows the delicious food.)

(Sorry that their temporary physical bond is about to end, they hold on to it for as long as they can...)

(CHE's words are meant to break the awkward spell.)

CHE: Your father died.

JULIA: Five years ago.

CHE: You don't have to talk about it if you don't...

JULIA: We were in the middle of building this school. A man who was never sick a day in his life. There were times when everyone in La Higuera would have a stomach virus or a fever...not Papi. *(Beat)* We were working on the roof. Almost finished. It was the last thing we had to do before putting down the floor. We announced an opening date and there was lots of excitement, though, as I said, some thought the school would ruin the kids, make 'em disrespectful and lazy. The sun was right above us. He was carrying the palm leaves up a ladder. Five straight hours of this. He stopped. Turned to me...in his eyes was such violence... like something inside was wrestling with his soul...it was the first time I ever saw him lose a fight. He said, "Julín, finish it." And fell. *(Beat)* My sister wanted to tear this building down with her bare hands— "First it took his sanity, then his health, now his life!" While my sister screamed, I finished the school myself, with the help of—of a friend. Climbed that ladder and put up the last of the roof.

CHE: And in my ignorance, I called it a prison. I'm so sorry.

JULIA: You don't have to say that. I'm sorry I didn't bring more to eat.

CHE: I don't think I ever had a more delicious meal.

JULIA: Oh—and my father was a wonderful cook!

CHE: Jesus Christ—you're right—I don't see how any man can compete with that!

JULIA: He had the power to change the way you breathe. Did you ever know anyone like that?

CHE: Only two. Fidel. And my mother. She more than he.

JULIA: Men don't usually say that about their mothers.

CHE: She said ideas were the greatest weapons—they burn everything in their path, then make something new from the fire. She taught us to deeply feel any injustice committed against anyone, anywhere in the world. That, in universal matters, each of us, alone, is worth nothing. But together? Well! *(Beat)* I've been lucky. I've had conversations with Beauvoir, Sartre, Mao, Nasser...no one kicks my fucking ass in an intellectual argument like my mother! Sorry, I said "fucking ass."

JULIA: I must be getting used to it.

CHE: One of the saddest days of my life was the day I was in Africa and I got word that she died. I felt as if... everything that connected me to Argentina was split that day. Cut with a knife. And I was truly homeless.

(Beat)

JULIA: Are you afraid?

CHE: Do you think it matters what I feel?

JULIA: You're not a face on a piece of currency. You're a man. Men feel.

CHE: I never should have been captured. I should have died in battle.

JULIA: Then it would have been all over.

CHE: Exactly. Now my story continues. Even if they execute me. They have my body to do whatever the fuck—whatever they want. They'll display me and say I died begging for my life, cursing Fidel, wetting my pants.

JULIA: But I'll know. I'll remember. *(Beat)* I'll fucking remember, Che.

(Beat)

CHE: If my hands were free...

(JULIA *makes the sign of the cross over* CHE.)

(CHE *looks at* JULIA, *silent, intense.*)

JULIA: What?

CHE: I think you should be married.

JULIA: You sound like my sister!

CHE: Don't laugh, marriage is a good thing for some people.

JULIA: Sorry, but I don't think you're a good spokesman for marriage.

CHE: What are you talking about? I was an exemplary husband. Twice. I was! When I was around...

JULIA: Uh-huh.

CHE: ...when I had the time, I gave my wife and children an example to follow. Tried to live up to my own rhetoric and ideals. That's not insignificant.

JULIA: Just boring.

CHE: Did you just call me "boring"?

JULIA: Che, what about love? Did you love your wife? Did you kiss Aleida's eyes? Did you soothe her when she woke up from a nightmare?

CHE: When I was around. I did what I could do. With the limited time and energy I had. That's all I can say.

(JULIA *looks away—not quite able to look in his eyes as she tells him this.*)

JULIA: I, uh, once had a "boyfriend." Maceo Marin Palacios. The "friend" who helped us build the school. Big dark hands, rough like wood from a tree. I touched them a couple of times. You'd think his rough fingers would be repulsive—but I'd see him and I'd want to sing. I'd work on the school all day, singing to myself like an idiot! Papi knew. I wanted Maceo Marin Palacios to worship me. To adore every inch of me. And know, really know— (*Indicates her body*) —this— all this...so if he closed his eyes he could describe me, inch by inch, to a blind man who would see me perfectly in the black theatre of his mind. (*Catches herself, smiles.*) My God, what am I going on about?

CHE: I don't mind.

JULIA: What's the point? Worship? Maceo? That hungry little man with the simple-minded wife and two sick kids? For a few months we worked side-by-side in silence. I touched his hands exactly twice. And I waited for a response that would change my life. He looked at me and those eyes burned for something...there was desire, I think ... or maybe I just invented it...an idiot girl who always seems to fall for married men...

CHE: Has he died?

JULIA: No. I see him almost every day. And nothing happens between us. I teach his kids who are sincere, but slow and sad. And I go on like this...un-worshipped, opinionated...too busy and intimidating to land a husband...a thoroughly difficult woman in a world of very weak men.

CHE: You could always marry the gallant and handsome Lieutenant Ramos.

(JULIA *laughs.*)

JULIA: My dear God, can you imagine?

CHE: I know from experience that the Cubans are pretty good at, well, you know...

JULIA: Ay! And the babies we'd make?

(*Beat. Then—*)

(JULIA *leans in quickly—and kisses* CHE *lightly on the cheek.*)

(*It's hard to tell which of them is more surprised by this.*)

CHE: I've got you cursing and kissing married men. In just two days. That's what I call a teacher.

JULIA: I am so sorry. I didn't come here to do that.

CHE: Maybe you did. And maybe you shouldn't punish yourself.

JULIA: No? Really? Good Catholic girl that I am?

CHE: What would we do without the Catholic Church keeping the world supplied with guilt and shame?

JULIA: I'm now resisting the urge to cross myself!

(JULIA *looks at him, deciding whether or not to divulge a secret.*)

I've been lying to everyone. I had a million noble reasons, having to do with the honor of this town, to see you. I wanted to see you because, well, because you're Che Guevara!

CHE: If I had the chance to meet Che Guevara, I'd take it too!

(JULIA *looks silently at* CHE, *as if trying to solve a puzzle about him.*)

JULIA: Oh God, it's just—with you, I get so...

CHE: With me, what?

JULIA: I don't get how a man like you...cultured and kind...tender, almost ... but you're a soldier, a war machine. You get up in the morning to kill. And they say you're merciless and brutal. Yet I look at you, and I don't...when I pictured the kind of man I'd...

CHE: How do you love a killer? Is that what you're asking?

JULIA: Why do you say love?

CHE: I don't know. It's not a word I like to throw around.

JULIA: I don't believe you. I bet you love everything. You love sunsets. You love water. You love music.

CHE: Actually, I'm tone deaf. Can't keep a beat.

JULIA: You love love itself. And because of that love, the world has opened itself up to you, and said, "You, sir, are different. You can take any path you want. Success waits for you everywhere." Yet with all those choices, you chose war.

CHE: War chose me.

JULIA: And you answered so quickly! You couldn't wait to give that awful mistress your blood and the blood of others. And who suffered? The family that misses you. Poor men like Willi. Countless souls who have died in all your struggles. And you, Che—your poor soul has suffered too—

CHE: "God," and "soul"—two of my least favorite words!

JULIA: A lot of people out there hate you. I know you know. And what sickness does to the body, hate does to the soul.

CHE: But you don't understand, every face of war, even the worst, has two sides.

JULIA: There's only one soul in you, Che, and you let it get, I don't know, corrupted—

CHE: One day, yes, you're impaling your enemy— a man who just happened to grow up on the opposite side of the border. The next, you're giving his children candy and water!

JULIA: And that isn't a kind of madness?

CHE: Of course it is. It's all madness. Nations, tribes, religions—different chapters in one great human book of madness.

JULIA: It's such a waste! Why should a good man like you be part of that? Why couldn't you work for peace with the same intensity?

CHE: Jesus fucking Christ, Julia, there is no peace for the kind of enemy I'm fighting! Do you think my enemy knows mercy? Don't you think they are capable of raping the innocent? Of flaying alive their captives? Or dropping chemicals on any man with brown skin? How was I supposed to fight that, Julia? To fight the greatest enemy of mankind: the United States of America. *(Beat)* I was brutal to the brutal. I met madness with equal madness. I drank as much blood as I could drink because I knew one day they'd be drinking mine. That's the contract we have with each other. That's what we depend on to give our existence meaning. And that's the only life that means anything to me.

(JULIA *looks at* CHE, *a little frightened, recoiling at his savage language.*)

JULIA: It just—don't be angry—it just breaks my heart to know this about you.

(Beat)

CHE: Julia—dear Julia—it's too late now. You can't convert me. Shape me like clay into some other form, something easier to live with and accept. If you've fallen in love with me...I mean, I'm sorry, if our friendship upsets you...then that's something you need—

JULIA: Am I alone?

CHE: What do you mean?

JULIA: Am I the only one—upset—by our friendship?

CHE: What do you think?

JULIA: I think you're not answering my question.

CHE: Julia. How can I answer it?

JULIA: Well, I'll tell you honestly, I don't think I'm alone. I can't be.

CHE: Then that's your answer. So let's leave it.

JULIA: Yes. All right. If that's all you can say.

CHE: Goddamn you—stop looking at me that way!

JULIA: What way?

CHE: Like I've disappointed you! I hate that look!
My mother was a master of it and so was Aleida!
And my daughters! Drives me nuts!

JULIA: I thought you said you didn't mind being judged.

CHE: Actually, it makes me crazy. *(Beat)* Yes, I could've
done many other things with my life, but I didn't.
I broke the hearts of two good women and five
beautiful kids. I led men and women to their deaths.
And what have I gotten for my struggles and
compromises—besides a corrupted soul, as you say?

JULIA: I'm sorry; that didn't come out right...

CHE: Faces and stories, Julia. Several lifetimes of faces
and stories. There's the face of the confused farmer
who sees your column approach, and he hasn't had a
stranger on his land in years. And your guns scare him
and his toothless wife is sure you're sorcerers out to
steal their one pathetic pig. And you talk to him about
freedom and Marx and the proletarian struggle and he
shakes his head because he doesn't know he's in a
struggle against any other force but the naked earth
itself. And all the time he wants you to leave him alone,
to the unchanging stubborn land that's his birthplace,
his prison, and his grave. *(Beat)* There's the face of the
ecstatic crowd, as you ride into the capital city, sitting
on a captured tank, and the world's cameras are on
you, and the dictator has fled, and it's New Years Day,
and the *yanquis* are astonished, and the Soviets have
not yet corrupted your vision, and along the narrow
streets are young men dying to join your triumph, and
beautiful young girls throwing flowers, and something
sacred, yes, I'll even use the word "God" un-ironically—
something like God has touched these hopeless people,
and freedom is swift and tangible, and at that moment
you know why you were born. *(Beat)* Then there's the

face of your dead friend...the boy who grew up in a rural town and never dreamed that history was going to sweep him up and put him at your side, in this grand universal struggle, and his loyalty is brutal, and his sacrifices too many to count, and you love this skinny little boy, you love that he's read every book you recommended, and went without food for you in the jungle, and believes, believes in his passionate rural heart, that the struggle is worth every minute of pain and dread you've inflicted on him. And when he dies and he looks at you with those fading eyes and he doesn't blame you, in fact, in his dying moment he loves you more than ever, and he whispers your name in his final pain and desperate animal panic, and he thanks you—then you know what war is about. You know what you can never fully teach another living person. *(Beat)* Last, there's the face of defeat, a face worse than the face of death, when your enemies are as big as gods, and your humiliation is total, and death seems like a sweet escape...that's my face, Julia. That's the face Ramos captured in his camera yesterday, the last my children and my comrades will ever see of me. *(He falls silent...)*

JULIA: Ask them for mercy. Demand it. Che, you want to live. You want to see Aleida again, and your kids. You want to live to fight again...

CHE: Do I? Do I really?

JULIA: What do you mean?

CHE: I made so many goddamn mistakes on this campaign—it's like I wanted them to capture me.

JULIA: You don't believe that.

CHE: Please don't make me out to be more than I am. I'm a small, failed, stupid man...

JULIA: Even like this, I've never seen anyone so strong and—

CHE: Worship the struggle, Julia, worship the promise of change—but don't worship me—or any of the petty men and women who pretend to lead you...

JULIA: If you could only know how you affect people—even your enemies—

CHE: Bullshit! I'm a goddamn joke! Do you know why I chose Bolivia? Because it's in the center of the continent. And I thought I could export a world-shaking revolution north, south, east, and west. All with a handful of scared young men! And you know why I thought I could do that? Because Fidel did it. With a couple of men, he changed a hemisphere. But he had one thing I never found here and will never find in a hundred years: the support of the people. I'd march into these towns and try to talk to people about land re-distribution and social justice and cooperative farming—and half of them didn't speak Spanish! And there I was—Ernesto Guevara Lynch telling these dark, ancient people how to live their lives. What choice did they have but to betray me to the Army?

JULIA: Che, please, it's not your fault—

CHE: I should have at least learned their language! If I wasn't so fucking arrogant and—

JULIA: It could take our people a hundred years to really understand....

CHE: You haven't had a hundred years and I bet you've changed more minds in an afternoon than I've done all year.

JULIA: You don't know how I've failed here! You don't know!

CHE: All year in Bolivia, I kept a journal of everything I thought and felt. Here's something I didn't write. Because I was too ashamed. It was a particularly bad day when we were running low on ammunition and medicine, morale was pure shit, the asthma was killing me. We hadn't recruited a single Bolivian peasant that month. My men were reduced to eating birds and monkeys and drinking their own urine. Then my horse panicked on the trail and nearly threw me. And I jumped off the poor creature and pulled out my knife—and before I knew what I was doing—I stabbed it in the chest—over and over again, Julia—there was so much fucking blood!—it was crazy!—all I wanted to do was kill everyone who betrayed us—every fucking hard-headed Bolivian in this fucking, hopeless country—then it got its blood in my eyes and mouth— I fucking swallowed it!—I was in—a rage—in a blind horrendous fucking— *(He has to struggle hard to keep control over himself—tears of rage threaten him)* —Until my men pulled me from the screaming animal. And I suddenly felt—so sorry for it. I tried to pat his head! Can you believe that? With my bloody hands. I stroked his head, crying like a fool, until he died. And I never once cried for any man I lost. *(Beat)* This is the kind of man you want to love? *(Beat)* Ultimately the horse got his own revenge: from that day on, I had to walk.

(JULIA wipes the tears on CHE's face.)

CHE: Ramos came in last night. Stinking drunk. Told me he'd prefer to rescue me. "Fuck Johnson! Fuck Barrientos!" But he's afraid of making a big historical mistake. Like Batista, when he set Fidel and Raul free. So he can't save me.

JULIA: What if someone else...?

CHE: He says the North Americans want to keep me alive to interrogate me. The final irony of my life is that I might end up in Cuba—in a prison in Guantanamo

Bay! And you know what's incredible? Neither Fidel nor Brezhnev nor Mao have enough power to stop them.

(JULIA *gets closer to* CHE.)

JULIA: I can get you out of here.

CHE: My girl...even if you could, we wouldn't get very far.

JULIA: I know every young man in La Higuera. They owe me! They'd help us!

CHE: And when they caught you...no, I've seen what enraged soldiers do to civilian women.

JULIA: I didn't sleep much last night. I stayed awake half the night thinking about this.

CHE: You say one more word, Cortes, and I will call the Lieutenant in here myself.

JULIA: If there's a chance...

CHE: The only chance I have is the mercy of President Barrientos. But not you. You can keep teaching. Keep trying to raise these kids above the goddamn mud the system keeps throwing at them. There's heroism in that. No less profound and necessary than a soldier's.

JULIA: Don't...

CHE: I've been lucky. Here. In this shithole. Surrounded by death. Fate has given me you—one, last, lovely inspiration.

JULIA: Don't lie to me.

CHE: You have everything you need to change this country. Tomorrow morning, you're going to dry your—those pretty eyes—and walk outside and, if you have to, pull every student in La Higuera out of their houses by the ears, and make them sit and understand that the simple fact that they are human beings, not dumb beasts as they've been taught all their lives, that that simple fact is the most powerful in the world. And you will change them. And this school will finally be a school. And never be a prison again.

(JULIA *is barely audible. Struggles not to cry*)

JULIA: Why do you lie to me...?

CHE: Look, I don't want to die. But I'm not afraid of leaving this world, or leaving behind the words and memories of the ones who hate me, or entering whatever void or silence that's waiting. My death will not hold back the march of revolution in Latin America. I know I will not outlive my ideas: I will fertilize them with my blood. *(Beat)* I'm only afraid of your sorrow, Julia. Try to find me where you can. Please—not in something as romantic and ridiculous as the damn sunset! No. Look for me, if you can, in the bright, clear things you see in the eyes of those kids you love so much.

JULIA: Its all a lie... *(She cries openly.)* I'm a fraud. I hate this school. I hate every stone in it. I hate coming here every morning. Hate the indifference in their eyes. The awful suspicion that maybe the last thing these boys and girls need is an education that leaves them dissatisfied with their lives. It's why it looks the way it is. Unfinished, broken, because I don't have the heart to try any more. I've lost my love for it. I'd much rather have a husband and my own kids! No. This school killed my father, it's killed my spirit, and now it's killing you.

(CHE *looks at* JULIA *with genuine pity and compassion.*)

CHE: Come closer.

(JULIA *comes closer to* CHE—*and gently rests her head on his chest. After a few quiet moments—*)

(The door opens.)

(FELIX *appears, looking pale, shaken, and trying not to show it.*)

(*His entrance startles* JULIA *and* CHE. *She pulls away from* CHE.)

JULIA: Jesus, that wasn't ten minutes!

FELIX: No, it was more like thirty. Let's go, Cortes.

JULIA: What happened? What did they decide?

FELIX: We're not fucking around here.

(FELIX *lifts* JULIA *roughly.*)

(*The* FIRST *and* SECOND ARMY RANGERS *appear at the door.*)

(CHE *struggles against his ropes.*)

CHE: RAMOS!

JULIA: What's going to happen to him?

(FELIX *pushes* JULIA *toward the door.*)

(*The* ARMY RANGERS *grab* JULIA.)

(*Before she can turn around to look at* CHE, *they pull her out of the school house and close the door.*)

CHE: I'll tear your fucking heart out for touching her!

(FELIX *waits for* CHE *to subside.*)

FELIX: Easy. EASY.

(CHE *is motionless.*)

(FELIX *takes out a knife, goes to* CHE, *and cuts the ropes around his wrists and feet.* CHE's *hands and legs are free for the first time since his capture.*)

CHE: What is this?

(*Free of bondage* CHE *struggles painfully to his feet.*)

FELIX: Two years ago I went to the C I A with a plan to kill your buddy Castro. They liked it. They liked me. I was very likeable back then. They gave me a nice, new rifle from Germany with a telescope on top. Told me about a house in Havana where Fidel liked to hang out. And the house nearby where I would hide and shoot and make history. They put me on a fast boat in Miami and, at night, we crossed over to my dear, wounded Cuba. But our contact failed to arrive. This happened three nights in a row. The contact never came. The C I A took my nice, new rifle away and said they changed their minds. You can understand my disappointment.

CHE: I don't give a shit...

FELIX: And here we are. The three of us. He's fat and happy in the dictatorial hell he's created on that island. And you're here, still fighting for him like a fool. And I'm in the middle. Che. Where's he been this whole time? Why hasn't he helped you? Sent money or men or support in an entire year? He wouldn't order your assassination...that's too crude, even for him. He'd just send you out to the jungle...

CHE: I sent myself here! It was my choice!

FELIX: ...with a half-emaciated army and two rusty guns and his borrowed ideology and let you die slowly from a lack of friends.

CHE: Listen to me, you fool. The shit you smell comes from Moscow, not Havana. In a country wracked by strikes and an active communist party, you'd think I'd get support. But I got nothing. If the Bolivian Communists raised one finger on my behalf, we wouldn't be here right now.

FELIX: We're alone, Che. Look, no recording devices on me. No one taking notes. Tell me, once and for all, you know Castro betrayed you. That if you had the chance— if you knew what he was really doing to the people of

that gorgeous land—that you, personally, would've
met me at the beach and taken me to that Havana
rendezvous and helped me put a nice German bullet
in his head.

CHE: Cuba's the first free territory of the Americas—
that's what really sickens you!

FELIX: Fuck!

(FELIX *pulls out his revolver and points it at* CHE.)

CHE: Do whatever you're going to do, you damn
coward. I'm just a man.

FELIX: You are. Just not the one I really wanted to get.
(Regaining control of himself, he holsters his gun.) I'm
sorry, Che. I did everything I could, spent most of
the night radioing everyone I could at the State
Department...but a couple of men just arrived from
the Bolivian High Command and they are not here as
tourists...

*(Fully understanding what's about to happen to him,
the color seems to drain from* CHE's *face.)*

CHE: Yes. It's better like this.

FELIX: Do you have any messages for your family?

CHE: Tell Fidel he will soon see a triumphant revolution
in America. Tell my wife to forget this and re-marry
and try to be happy. And tell my children to study hard
and be good revolutionaries.

(Impressed with CHE's *courage,* FELIX *steps toward him.)*

FELIX: You are what they said you'd be.

(FELIX *embraces* CHE.)

(Surprised, but understanding, CHE *holds him.)*

(Unable to look at CHE *any longer,* FELIX *leaves.)*

(CHE *is alone.)*

(He looks around at the dark, silent school house. The last place he'll ever know. Stumbles to the blackboard and erases:)

CHE: *Vosotros huid.*

(Black out)

END OF ACT THREE

ACT FOUR

Scene One

(Half hour later)

(JULIA's house)

(LUCILA has made lunch.)

(LUCILA and JULIA sit at the table in silence, food between them.)

(LUCILA eats, worried to death about JULIA.)

(Preoccupied, JULIA can't touch her food.)

(The long silence is too much for LUCILA.)

LUCILA: Helicopters! God! They're just crazy, you know? Why don't they have wings? How do they stay up?

JULIA: I don't know, Lu...

LUCILA: At one time they would've called that magical. A thing that stays up in the air without wings! Angels and spirits must be holding it up! But today? In this Godless world? It isn't angels that hold things up in the air, it's science! Science my ass!

JULIA: Of course it's science.

LUCILA: Julia. I said "ass" and you didn't even blink.

(JULIA thinks a moment before she can respond.)

JULIA: Sometimes, Lu, for some reasons known only to God...He decides to bring the whole world to your door...with all its noises, its dreams, its gorgeous monsters...and manages to quietly crush everything you know. Why would He do that?

LUCILA: Look, angel, there are other men in the world...

JULIA: Oh stop, you have no idea what you're talking about...

LUCILA: I know my romantic sister!

JULIA: You think all I do is think with my heart! That there aren't other organs in me fed with something other than blood and tears...

LUCILA: I know you better than you know you.

JULIA: Ay, just leave me alone!

LUCILA: I won't because I see you wasting away here. You think all I do is think about myself. All right, I do think about myself a lot—but I notice things. You're getting old here. Teaching blind little kids to see, deaf little monsters to hear. And no one says thanks. I don't want that for you. I want you to find some life.

JULIA: I found some life and a bunch of soldiers have their guns aimed at it!

LUCILA: It's no good. Don't fall in love with a ghost.

(JULIA *angrily leaves the table.*)

JULIA: God, this room is a PRISON!

LUCILA: Yes! And you need to get out. That's what I'm saying. But not with a man who is not of your world—

JULIA: You don't know a thing about this!

LUCILA: Don't take me for a fool. Don't disrespect me like that. *(Beat)* Maceo came by today and I know what's in his heart, even if it never comes out of his mouth...

JULIA: It finally happened. You've finally lost your mind.

LUCILA: Everyone in La Higuera knows! That his marriage is a joke. Rosa Anna says his kids aren't his! That there's only been one woman for him!

JULIA: Me and Maceo!

LUCILA: At least he's real.

JULIA: After today, Lu, there's no way. You know why I never made a move for him? Because I knew Papi would look down on it, not because of the infidelity, but because that little coward didn't deserve me.

LUCILA: You're so stuck up. No wonder you're alone.

JULIA: Stuck up and proud of it. And sick of all this crap!

LUCILA: Then you gotta leave La Higuera. Don't stay for me and waste away. I can live with that sweet, nice Rosa Anna and she'll take care of me. If the great world has crushed your love of this town—and the people here—what else can you do? Go out—find someone to respect. And may God use his good magic to turn that respect into love.

JULIA: But if I go, who'll teach the kids?

LUCILA: If you stay, who'll teach you?

(No answer from JULIA for a moment.)

JULIA: What does the radio say?

LUCILA: I've been too scared to turn it on.

JULIA: Times like these demand some courage, Sis. *(She turns on the radio.)*

FIRST RADIO VOICE: ...for the countryside. Our peasantry is resourceful. They are proud and even if they're not well-educated, they possess an instinctive canniness. In fact it could be argued that the peasant's native brilliance, his closeness to God, his close family bonds, his love of the land, his innate understanding of the animal and plant world...

JULIA: Listen to this romantic bullshit!

FIRST RADIO VOICE: ...makes it largely unnecessary to invest great amounts of money in his "formal" education, money that could be better used in the cities...

JULIA: Money that could be better spent lining the pockets of President Barrientos!

FIRST RADIO VOICE: ...money for infrastructure— bridges, railroads, sewer lines—money for the kind of projects...

LUCILA: Turn it off if it's gonna give you a heart attack!

FIRST RADIO VOICE: ...that promote industry and ensure the prosperity of all—

(An abrupt silence on the radio.)

(A SECOND *RADIO VOICE comes on suddenly—)*

SECOND RADIO VOICE: Ladies and gentlemen, there is now some information coming in to Radio Pio Doce from the vicinity of La Higuera, the bucolic little hamlet where so much of the country's attention has turned for the last two days. We are now getting reports— are these confirmed? Do we have confir—? *(Beat)* This report is not officially confirmed but, apparently bears the weight of some authority: we have learned that the Argentine Marxist Ernesto Che Guevara was killed in combat today, five miles outside La Higuera.

JULIA: They're lying!

SECOND RADIO VOICE: Soldiers of the newly-minted Second Ranger Battalion surrounded the guerilla infiltrator at ten o'clock this morning and, in a fierce fire fight lasting three hours, Guevara was shot in battle and pronounced dead only moments ago, on the battlefield...

(A distant gun shot)

(Another)

(JULIA and LUCILA are frozen.)

SECOND RADIO VOICE: Officers on the scene have confirmed, only provisionally, the facts we have just—

(In her fury, JULIA grabs the radio and hurls it against the wall. Then falls to the ground in a heap of silent curses.)

(LUCILA goes to JULIA and holds her a long moment.)

LUCILA: Dear God, in all your mercy, look down upon my little sister and cleanse her tears, relieve her burning wounds, give her lasting peace and let her carry her memories to a gentle grave with grace and tranquility.

(As LUCILA holds JULIA, we hear the sound of a helicopter's engine starting...then the blades begin to turn...going faster and faster, nearly shaking apart the fragile house.)

(Black out)

Scene Two

(That night)

(Inside the school house)

(A few candles on the floor and desks provide the only light.)

(CHE's blood is still visible on the walls and dirt floor.)

(FELIX sits at one of the desks staring at his hands, drinking, wheezing slightly.)

(JULIA appears at the doorway.)

JULIA: Where is he?

FELIX: They flew his body to Vallegrande.

JULIA: You didn't go with him?

FELIX: Not enough room in the chopper. Colonel Joaquin Zenteno Anaya, Commander of the Eighth Army Division and Colonel Arnaldo Sauredo, an intelligence chief, hogged up the only available seats. So guess who's going to be walking to Vallegrande tomorrow. Drink?

JULIA: Did you shoot him?

FELIX: Several of the guys wanted to do the honors. It went to a stupid little sergeant named Mario Teran who was chosen for a good, humanitarian reason: it was his birthday today.

JULIA: How do you live with yourself, Lieutenant?

FELIX: I asked Teran not to shoot Che in the face. I didn't want to make it too hard to identify him. I think they plan to amputate his hands and send them to Buenos Aires to check against his fingerprints...

JULIA: Stop talking. I can't stand the sound of your voice, Ramos.

(Beat)

FELIX: Rodriguez.

(Beat)

JULIA: Is there nothing you don't lie about?

FELIX: It's my job, Miss. *(He takes a long drink.)*

(Then FELIX and JULIA endure the silence of the small school house. The only sound: FELIX's very audible wheezing.)

(JULIA looks at him.)

JULIA: Is that you?

FELIX: It started as soon as they took him away.
The craziest thing. I've never had asthma in my life.
Now it won't stop.

(*The sound of* FELIX's *breathing is so reminiscent of* CHE's...)

(JULIA *cries quietly.*)

(*It's hard to tell if she's talking to* FELIX *or to the spot where* CHE *died.*)

JULIA: Before we built this school, we had to walk all
the way to Villa Piedad for an education. But my father
believed in education for all—even the poor. And he
knew that a lot of our kids were living in ignorance
because they couldn't walk the thirteen miles. He was
old and the one thing he wanted to do in life was bring
a school to this town. Even if it killed him. (*She kneels
to touch the bloody place where* CHE *died.*) In the morning,
I'm going to get some of the able-bodied men and
women of La Higuera together. And we're going to
put a floor down. And we're going to paint these walls
and wash the old dirt off the windows. Get some of the
new school supplies Barrientos keeps bragging about.
And a great school is going to be born right here...
I promise you...

(FELIX *looks at her, his asthma loud and getting louder,
as if to suffocate him.*)

(*Fade to black*)

END OF PLAY

www.ingramcontent.com/pod-product-compliance
Lightning Source LLC
Chambersburg PA
CBHW070025110426
42741CB00034B/2558